Jan. 19, 2010

D1327214

Transcending Race in America
Biographies of Biracial Achievers

Halle Berry

Beyoncé

David Blaine

Mariah Carey

Frederick Douglass

W. E. B. Du Bois

Salma Hayek

Derek Jeter

Alicia Keys

Soledad O'Brien

Rosa Parks

Prince

Booker T. Washington

DAVID BLAINE

Illusionist and Endurance Artist

Chuck Bednar

Mason Crest Publishers

Produced by 21st Century Publishing and Communications, Inc.

MASON CREST PUBLISHERS INC.
370 Reed Road
Broomall, Pennsylvania 19008
(866) MCP-BOOK (toll free)
www.masoncrest.com

Printed in the United States of America.

First Printing

9 8 7 6 5 4 3 2 1

Library of Congress Cataloging-in-Publication Data

Bednar, Chuck, 1976–
    David Blaine : illusionist and endurance artist / Chuck Bednar.
        p. cm. — (Transcending race in America : biographies of biracial achievers)
    Includes bibliographical references and index.
    ISBN 978-1-4222-1609-5 (hardback : alk. paper) — ISBN 978-1-4222-1623-1 (pbk. : alk. paper)
    1. Blaine, David, 1973– 2. Magicians—United States—Biography. I. Title.
GV1545.B57A3 2010
793.8092—dc22
[B]   2009022041

Table of Contents

> **"** I HAVE BROTHERS, SISTERS, NIECES,
> NEPHEWS, UNCLES, AND COUSINS,
> OF EVERY RACE AND EVERY HUE,
> SCATTERED ACROSS THREE CONTINENTS,
> AND FOR AS LONG AS I LIVE,
> I WILL NEVER FORGET THAT
> IN NO OTHER COUNTRY ON EARTH
> IS MY STORY EVEN POSSIBLE. **"**

> **"** WE MAY HAVE DIFFERENT STORIES,
> BUT WE HOLD COMMON HOPES. . . .
> WE MAY NOT LOOK THE SAME
> AND WE MAY NOT HAVE
> COME FROM THE SAME PLACE,
> BUT WE ALL WANT TO MOVE
> IN THE SAME DIRECTION —
> TOWARDS A BETTER FUTURE . . . **"**

— BARACK OBAMA, 44TH PRESIDENT
OF THE UNITED STATES OF AMERICA

Chapter

1

❖

A
RECORD-SETTING
PERFORMANCE

ON APRIL 30, 2008, THE SPELLBOUND AUDIENCE of *The Oprah Winfrey Show* fixed their eyes on a giant water-filled sphere, not unlike a snow globe. Inside was David Blaine, world-famous magician and performer of physical endurance feats. He floated, all but motionless, as he attempted to set the world record in the breath-holding category.

This was not David's first attempt at the record. In May 2006, he was **submerged** for a week in a similar sphere, with tubes coming in for air and liquid food. There he had attempted to break the record for holding his breath, but he was brought up one minute and fifty seconds short of his goal after assistants began fearing for his health. Since that time, a new record had been established. In February 2008, a Swiss man named Peter

David Blaine floats motionless underwater as he sets a world record for breath-holding before a live audience on *The Oprah Winfrey Show*, April 30, 2008. David's amazing and dangerous feats of physical endurance have made history and continue to fascinate his fans worldwide.

Colat held his breath underwater for 16 minutes, 32 seconds. That time became David's target in the days and weeks leading up to April 30, as he strived once again to make history.

David takes a final breath before going underwater and holding his breath for a record 17 minutes, 4 seconds. To prepare for the event, David trained with Navy SEALs, practiced breath holds every day, and slept in a special device that got his lungs used to less-than-normal oxygen levels.

Other Famous Breath Holders

There have been many individuals besides David and Peter Colat who achieved incredible feats of breath holding. Germany's Tom Sietas, for example, was the man whose record Colat broke in February 2008. In September, following David's record-setting feat on *The Oprah Winfrey Show*, Sietas appeared on *Live with Regis and Kelly* and set another new record (17 minutes, 19 seconds).

Sietas also owns the mark for the longest time holding his breath without the use of oxygen beforehand (10 minutes, 12 seconds). Giancarlo Bellingrath of Italy owns the record for the longest total time spent holding his breath over the course of an hour (59 minutes, 45 seconds). Finally, Robert Foster of the United States managed to set a time of 13 minutes, 42 seconds while submerged in 10 feet of water.

PREPARING FOR THE BIG MOMENT

It wouldn't be an easy task to **surpass** Colat's record. David knew that a lot of training and hard work would be involved, and he prepared accordingly. He built up his tolerance to carbon dioxide by doing repeated breath holds each morning. For the month leading up to the stunt, David slept in a machine known as a hypoxic tent. This device was designed to simulate the high-altitude air of 15,000 feet, which contains less oxygen. As he told John Tierney of *The New York Times*, David got advice from free-diving coach Kirk Krack.

❝Kirk . . . taught me to relax into it. The stillness changes everything. It is much easier to go further when the condition is accepted instead of opposed. . . . I found out that by doing good cardio training and not eating foods for the sake of indulgence, but rather for the nutritional value, the body functions like a well maintained machine.❞

Prior to the event, in addition to the endurance training, David had the sphere he had used during his previous underwater breath-holding stunt shipped to Oprah's studio in Chicago. Then on the day of the attempt, just before entering the tank, he spent 23 minutes inhaling air through a breathing tube. This would **saturate** his lungs with oxygen, boosting his chances of success while remaining within the record-setting guidelines. Afterward, with the show's host and the audience watching, he was lowered into the water-filled sphere and the clock started.

Upon hitting the water, David attempted to clear his mind and relax, just as his coach had taught him. It wasn't easy, though, as a heart monitor, which was required to keep tabs on his condition, beeped steadily nearby. Oprah was joined by medical officials for a quiet, somewhat low-key commentary that continued throughout the stunt. It was time, as Oprah put it, to test "the limits of the human body."

MAKING HISTORY

The first eight minutes passed without incident, but there was always danger, as the lack of oxygen could damage David's heart and lungs. The goal was to lower his heart rate, which would make the stunt easier and less painful. During training, he had managed to get it down below 50 beats per minute, but during *The Oprah Winfrey Show*, it started at 130 and was only down to 124 by the 15-minute mark. The clock kept ticking, as David passed 16 minutes, then continued on past the old record of 16 minutes, 32 seconds.

With the record set, David remained submerged for another 30-plus seconds. When he finally did come to the surface, the clock displayed 17 minutes, 4 seconds. The record had fallen, and David Blaine had made history. Afterward, he described the experience:

> **"I really thought I was not going to make it. . . . At minute 12 I felt the pain coming, and by minute 14 it was overwhelming. This was a whole other level of pain. I still feel as if somebody hit me in the stomach with the hardest punch they could . . . [but] it's better when you have to fight, anyway."**

17:04.4

DAVID BLAINE

Even though David felt great pain during his endurance feat and medical personnel hovered nearby, he quickly recovered. After breaking the world breath-holding record, David told Oprah he felt great, and that his achievement was a life-long dream come true.

David had performed many amazing illusions and several incredible feats of physical endurance over the years. He had dazzled fans by doing things like burying himself alive and spending more than two full days encased in a block of ice. However, with this amazing stunt, he had set a world record and secured a place among the greatest performers of his era.

2

DRAWN TO MAGIC

LONG BEFORE HIS DRAMATIC APPEARANCE on *The Oprah Winfrey Show*, young David had been **enamored** with magic and performed feats of endurance as a child. The son of an Italian/Puerto Rican father and a Jewish mother of Russian origin, David devoted much of his childhood both to the art of illusion and the science of testing his physical limits.

David Blaine White was born on April 4, 1973. His father, William Perez, was a veteran of the Vietnam War who left the family when David was just a toddler. After that, his mother, Patrice Maureen White, raised him alone in Brooklyn, New York. David wrote in his book, *Mysterious Stranger: A Book of Magic*, he and his mother faced many difficulties during this time. Several apartment buildings in which they lived burned down, and Patrice worked three different jobs to raise money for David to attend a special school in New Jersey.

David has kept his early story something of a mystery, but his heritage is a mixture of Italian, Puerto Rican, and Russian backgrounds. He was drawn to magic at an early age because he was fascinated by the mystery and science behind the craft.

When David was 11, his mother married John Bukalo, and they moved to Little Falls, New Jersey, to live with his new stepfather and his stepbrother, Michael. David attended Passaic Valley High School there, but academics were not his major concern. By then, David's love affair with performance magic was beginning to blossom.

Multiracial Marriage in America

While these days, it might seem like no big deal to see a husband and wife of different races, this hasn't always been the case. In fact, for a long time, several states in the U.S. had laws restricting or banning multiracial marriage. That ended in 1967, however, with the Supreme Court's ruling in *Loving* v. *Virginia*.

In that landmark court case, Mildred Loving, a woman of mixed African and Native American heritage, sued the state of Virginia over a rule banning a marriage between a white person and an individual of any other racial background. The Supreme Court ruled in favor of Loving, stating that all race-based legal restrictions in America were unconstitutional. These days, nearly 5 percent of all marriages in the U.S. are multiracial, according to the most recent census bureau statistics.

DAVID'S INFLUENCES

So how did David first get involved with magic? In keeping with an old magician's code, he has worked hard to keep his story a mystery. Once he told a reporter that a cousin introduced him to the craft when he was just four years old. Another time, he said his mother bought him his first trick. His love for stunts supposedly comes from a time when he walked across a plank that connected two tall buildings, and he practiced holding his breath during swimming races at a local YMCA. In his book, David has this to say:

"You don't get into magic. Magic gets into you. I've been fascinated by the art for as long as I can remember. Part of my love for magic is about the mystery and science behind it. It also has to do about astonishment and control. It was as if my hands had an independent need to manipulate things."

Regardless of how he first gained his love for magic, young David was influenced by many people. Both illusionists and those from other walks of life inspired him. Uri Geller, Jean Eugène Robert-Houdin, and Harry Houdini were among his favorite magicians growing up. Other individuals who David

Growing up, David was influenced by famous figures like Martin Luther King Jr., Malcolm X, and Muhammad Ali. Equally inspiring were magicians Jean Eugène Robert-Houdin, Harry Houdini, and Uri Geller (shown here), who claims to be able to bend spoons with the power of his mind.

When David's mother died of cancer, he constantly worked at his magic as a way to get over the tragedy. Soon his dedication paid off. He began earning good money performing in night clubs, and he met several celebrities who later became his close friends.

says affected him as a child include Orson Wells, Martin Luther King, Jr., Malcolm X, Muhammad Ali, and Jesus Christ— "not necessarily in that order," as an interview with magic-directory.com points out.

DEDICATING HIMSELF TO HIS MAGIC

At the age of 17, David moved back to New York and worked as a street magician to raise the rent money for his apartment. However, while he began performing magic out of a love for the art and then started working at it professionally to pay the bills, he soon used it to overcome tragedy in his life. David's mother died from cancer when he was 19, and suddenly he felt alone in the world. As a result, as David told magicdirectory.com, he turned to magic for comfort.

> **"That was the worst thing that has happened in my life. I was standing there with nobody and nothing left. . . . So, I went full force ahead, doing magic everywhere, every single second, because that's all I really had!"**

Working as a street magician not only helped him fill the void left by the loss of his mother, but it also began to get him noticed. He and his friends would often wind up in night clubs, and eventually started earning as much as $300 per hour performing for famous individuals such as Christopher Walken, Robert DeNiro, and Leonardo DiCaprio. As longtime friend Adam Gibgot later told guardian.co.uk, the celebrities "would become his friend for life; he turned them into children again."

It was also during these types of shows that David met Ted Harbert, who at the time was the chairman of ABC Entertainment. Ted was impressed with David's talents—so impressed, in fact, that he convinced his television network to air a special featuring the 24-year-old magician. David Blaine was about to become a star.

Chapter
3

GREAT
MAGICIANS PAST
AND PRESENT

WHETHER YOU PREFER TO CALL THEM ILLUSION, sleight of hand, **prestidigitation**, **legerdemain**, escapology, or just plain old magic, the various arts performed by David Blaine can be traced back thousands of years. In fact, in his book, David writes that the first such performances are said to have taken place in Ancient Egypt some 5,000 years ago!

In 1584, an English author named Reginald Scot wrote a book called *Discoverie of Witchcraft*. While the book was largely written to address the believed practice of witchcraft during the medieval era, it also contained 22 pages devoted to the discussion of stage-style magic tricks. Stage shows featuring flame eaters, stone eaters, and individuals performing similar feats became fairly common in the 17th and 18th centuries, but it wasn't until the early 1800s that modern performance-style stage magic started to come about.

Although many of David's illusions seem new and modern, magic has been practiced for hundreds of years. In this painting, "The Magician," by 15th century Dutch painter Hieronymus Bosch, a fascinated crowd watches a conjurer perform the famous cups and balls trick.

"THE THREE MAGI"

In the third chapter of *Mysterious Stranger: A Book of Magic*, David writes about "The Three Magi," who were three men he claims "brought the art of magic to a new level." First is Jean Eugène Robert-Houdin, a French magician who lived from 1805 to 1871. Robert-Houdin is often referred to as the father of modern

One of the Three Magi who inspired David was Jean Eugène Robert-Houdin, a 19th century French magician called the father of modern stage magic. Houdin believed magicians should appear to have superhuman powers, a concept David has incorporated into his physical feats of endurance.

stage magic, and he became famous for performing mind-reading and **levitation** tricks that also featured his son, Emile.

In the book, David discusses his intense interest in Robert-Houdin's work:

> **"Robert-Houdin's theories of magic were what intrigued me the most. His notion that a magician is an actor who plays the part of someone with super-natural powers . . . made Robert-Houdin's magical effects among the most memorable ever performed."**

Another member of the Magi was Max Malini. Malini was born in Poland in 1873 and performed until his death in 1942. According to David's tales, Malini was well known for preparing tricks ahead of time. He once set up a future trick by visiting a tailor and hiding a playing card in the suit of a U.S. senator. Later, he disguised a living, featherless chicken as a cooked one, sedated it, and appeared to make it come back to life during a dinner party.

Rounding out the Three Magi is Alexander Herrmann, who lived from 1844 to 1896. David calls Herrmann "the complete magician," describing him as tall and thin, sporting a fancy moustache and always playing his onstage character. Herrmann could reportedly throw a card so well it would land in the lap of any audience member, and also successfully pulled off the "bullet catch" more than a half dozen times.

HARRY HOUDINI

While the contributions of the Three Magi to the world of magic and illusion were obviously important, they pale in comparison to those of the legendary Harry Houdini. Houdini, who was born Ehrich Weiss in Budapest, Hungary on March 24, 1874, is possibly the most famous magician and escape artist of all time. During his life, he performed sleight of hand and worked to expose fake psychics and spiritualists. However, as David points out in his book, Houdini is most remembered for his amazing escapes.

> **"Why do we still care about Houdini? I think part of the answer is that Houdini . . . was much more than a mere magician. . . . The biggest illusion Houdini created was his own myth—that he was . . . a modern-day Superman."**

Houdini accomplished many incredible feats during his life. In 1904, he escaped from a special set of handcuffs that had taken a locksmith over five years to create. He would regularly escape from a water-filled container—first a milk can, and later a device known as a Chinese Water Torture Cell, which required him to be chained at the feet and lowered upside down into a glass case. Houdini would regularly free himself from a straitjacket, and was also buried alive three times during his career. He died on Halloween, 1926.

The Legacy of Harry Houdini

Though Harry Houdini passed away in 1926, his legacy has lived on. Almost 30 years later, in 1953, the movie *Houdini* starring Tony Curtis was released, though it wasn't completely accurate in its portrayal of the magician's real life. Several other motion pictures and stage musicals followed, including the 1968 play *Man of Magic*, the 1976 made-for-TV film *The Great Houdinis*, the 1985 television movie *Young Harry Houdini*, and the 1998 cable TV movie *Houdini*.

His legacy extends beyond the film world, however. In 1968, the Houdini Hall of Fame was opened in Niagara Falls, Ontario, Canada. In 1975, he **posthumously** received a star on the Hollywood Walk of Fame. In 1976, singer, songwriter, and poet Patti Smith wrote "Ha! Ha! Houdini!" and other musicians, including Kate Bush, The Melvins, and Nick Cave & The Bad Seeds have released songs inspired by the famed escape artist. Also, in 2002, the U.S. Postal Service issued a stamp featuring an old Houdini promotional poster.

DOUG HENNING

While feats of illusion and prestidigitation were still being practiced following Houdini's death, the art form did show a lull in popularity until the 1970s, when it experienced a revival thanks to

Harry Houdini, another of David's heroes, was a legendary magician and escape artist. His most famous escapes were from specially made handcuffs, a milk can, and a straightjacket. Here Houdini is about to free his hands and feet from chains and escape from a stone-walled jail.

the efforts of Doug Henning. Henning was a Canadian performer who was born in 1947. He graduated from McMaster University with a psychology degree, and combined what he learned in school with his love of performance magic to create *Spellbound*, a musical play all about prestidigitation. *Spellbound* became

The Magic Show, which ran on Broadway from 1974 through 1978 and earned Henning a Tony Award nomination.

In 1975, he made his television debut with the NBC special *Doug Henning's World of Magic.* That special drew more than 50 million viewers and led to several others, as well as seven lifetime Emmy Award nominations. In one of his most famous illusions, he made an entire house appear to levitate. Growing up, Henning had also been a big fan of Houdini, performing Houdini's water chamber escape during his first NBC special and later writing a book about the magician's life. He died in February 2000, only a few months after being diagnosed with liver cancer.

MAGICIAN DAVID COPPERFIELD

One of the most famous magicians of the modern era is David Seth Kotkin, better known by his stage name, David Copperfield. Copperfield was born on September 16, 1956, in New Jersey. He began practicing magic as a preteen, and at the age of 12 became the youngest person ever admitted to the Society of American Magicians. By 16, he was teaching a course on prestidigitation at New York University, and in 1977, he hosted and starred in the first of more than two dozen career television specials.

Over the years, Copperfield has performed some of the most amazing and compelling illusions in the history of magic. In 1980, he made an automobile float in the air. One year later, he made an airplane disappear, and followed that up by making the Statue of Liberty vanish in 1983. In 1984, he appeared to float above the Grand Canyon, and in 1986, he seemingly walked through the Great Wall of China. In recent years, he has been performing for audiences in Las Vegas, which prompted casinoman.net to note:

66 Before Chris Angel and David Blaine came along . . . Copperfield reigned supreme as the top illusionist in the world. . . . He is hailed by both fans and critics alike as the greatest illusionist of all time. If you've never seen David Copperfield perform, there's no better time than right now. . . . He's truly one of a kind. 99

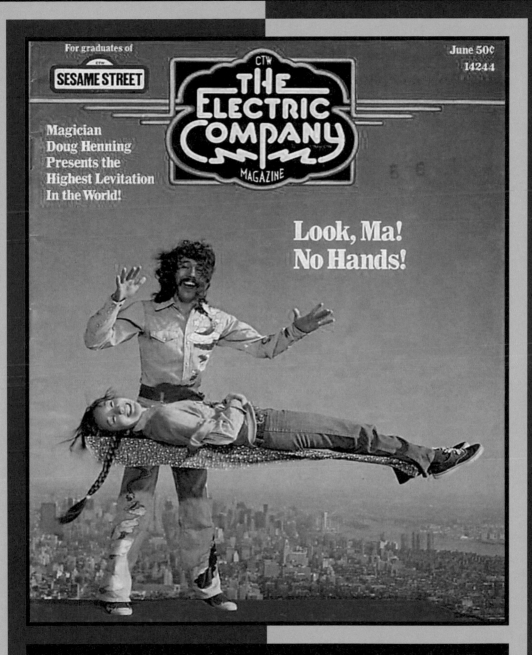

For graduates of
SESAME STREET

Magician
Doug Henning
Presents the
Highest Levitation
In the World!

June 50¢
14244

CTW
**THE
ELECTRIC
COMPANY**
MAGAZINE

Look, Ma!
No Hands!

Doug Henning helped performance magic regain its popularity in the 1970s.
One of his most famous illusions was making a house appear to levitate.
Henning gained many fans with his Broadway and television shows and
received seven lifetime Emmy nominations.

Copperfield is a five-time Emmy Award winner, and in 2003, he was one of the 10 highest-paid celebrities in the world, according to *Forbes* magazine. He has been presented with a Living Legend Award from the Library of Congress, and was the first living magician to be given a star on the Hollywood Walk of Fame. His Project Magic foundation promotes physical therapy

Magician David Copperfield promotes his new show "Grand Illusion" in 2009. He told reporters, "For magic to be relevant, it has to evolve so it keeps up with the best film and theater. I want to base my work on what people really dream about. Most of us don't dream of pulling a rabbit out of a hat."

David Copperfield the Book

David Copperfield, the magician, took his stage name from *David Copperfield*, the book. Written by Charles Dickens, the book tells the story of a young man named David Copperfield, who supposedly was based on the author himself. The book was first published in a series of 19 monthly installments from May 1849 through November 1850.

According to Cummings Study Guides, *David Copperfield* is a book about the power of love, the need to be optimistic, and the importance of working hard to overcome challenges. So was there some reason why the magician born David Seth Kotkin chose "David Copperfield" for his stage name? It is unlikely, considering that Copperfield has admitted that he has never read the book, telling Britannica Online Encyclopedia that it was "too dark" for him.

through sleight of hand in over 1,000 hospitals worldwide. He has also acted in a few movies, contributed to two collections of short stories, and was once engaged to model Claudia Schiffer.

OTHER MODERN MAGICIANS

David Blaine is just one of many popular illusionists and escape artists who have been performing in recent years. One of the most notable duos of all time was Siegfried & Roy, who mixed magic and animal training during their performances. In 1972, their show was named the best in Las Vegas, and in 1999, they were honored with a star on the Hollywood Walk of Fame. Their final show was on February 28, 2009.

Like Siegfried & Roy, Penn & Teller manage to combine magic with another entertainment style—in this case, comedy—in their performances. Penn & Teller have won numerous Emmy and Writers' Guild awards for their work and have written several books together as well. Other well-known magicians of today include Criss Angel, Derren Brown, Lance Burton, Paul Daniels, Ricky Jay, the Pendragons, and Val Valentino.

Chapter

4

THE HIP-HOP HOUDINI

IN THE LATE '90S, DAVID BLAINE BEGAN working to secure his place alongside the great magicians of the past. Before raising the stakes with incredible stunts such as burying himself alive or freezing himself in a giant block of ice, however, he started with a pair of old-school television magic shows: *David Blaine: Street Magic* and *David Blaine: Magic Man.*

Street Magic aired on May 19, 1997, and featured David performing card tricks and sleight of hand on the streets of New York. The show also featured appearances by a number of celebrities, including Leonardo DiCaprio, Spike Lee, and members of the Dallas Cowboys. Ted Harbert, the ABC executive who gave David his own television special, told *The New York Times* it was the magician's unique approach that sold him on the deal.

Watch closely... because you won't believe your eyes.

No smoke. No mirrors. No stage. Pure magic hits the streets.

DAVID BLAINE: STREET MAGIC

Monday, May 19 at 8/7c on abc

David's TV special, David Blaine: Street Magic, aired in 1997 and featured the magician performing legerdemain on the streets of New York. The show made magic accessible to audiences in fresh ways, and his streetwise personality gained him the nickname "The Hip-Hop Houdini."

In his early career and television shows, David had tried to bring magic back to its glory days of a hundred years ago. In the late 1990s he changed his focus, emphasizing feats of escapism and physical endurance such as those practiced by Houdini.

Leonardo DiCaprio

One of David's closest friends is actor Leonardo DiCaprio. Leonardo was born on November 11, 1974, and earned his first big break when he joined the cast of the television sitcom *Growing Pains* during its final season. In 1992, he co-starred in *This Boy's Life*, alongside Hollywood heavyweight Robert DeNiro. Leonardo's performance in the film earned him lots of attention and helped him launch a successful film career.

Hot on the heels of *This Boy's Life*, he starred in a series of films that were both popular and critically acclaimed, including *What's Eating Gilbert Grape*, *The Basketball Diaries*, *Romeo + Juliet*, *Titanic*, and *Blood Diamond*. He has been nominated for several Academy Awards and won a Golden Globe for his work in *The Aviator*. In 2008, Leonardo starred in *Body of Lies* and *Revolutionary Road*, and his upcoming films include *Ashecliffe* and *The Rise of Theodore Roosevelt*.

"We've seen magic specials before. This is a different way of presenting what may very well be the same kind of tricks. It's more accessible. He's taken a craft that's been around for hundreds of years and done something unique and fresh with it."

While David's star was already on the rise, *Street Magic* helped him reach the next level. In 1997, he had begun dating singer Fiona Apple. Later on, he began work on *Magic Man*, which

Fiona Apple

In 1997, David started dating singer Fiona Apple. Fiona was born in New York City on September 13, 1977. In 1994, she became involved in the music business in a rather creative way—she gave a demo tape to a friend who was the babysitter for a music publicist. That tape wound up in the hands of Sony Music officials, who signed her to a record deal and published her debut album, *Tidal*, in 1996.

Tidal made Fiona an immediate star. The album went on to sell more than 2.5 million copies, produced a Grammy-winning hit in "Criminal," and helped Fiona earn *Rolling Stone* magazine's 1997 Performer of the Year honors. In 2008, *Entertainment Weekly* named *Tidal* one of the 100 Best Albums of the Past 25 Years. She has since released two additional albums: 1999's *When the Pawn...* and 2005's *Extraordinary Machine*.

aired on April 14, 1999. Like his first special, *Magic Man* featured traditional-style illusions performed on an individual level. This time, however, he traveled to other U.S. cities, as well as Haiti and Venezuela. The show was watched by nearly 13 million viewers.

CHANGING HIS FOCUS

Both in the early part of his career and during the filming of his first two television specials, David had a mission. He was eager to return the art of illusion to its glory days. As he had once told *The New York Times*,

> **"**I'd like to bring magic back to the place it used to be 100 years ago. I like the way Houdini brought magic to the people on the streets, genuinely. . . . The reason for magic is to enlighten people or make them happy, or let them forget their problems for two minutes.**"**

Feeling that the original task had been accomplished, David then started to **aspire** to bigger and better things. Specifically, he wanted to get away from tricks like fixing torn playing cards, making coins disappear, and predicting numbers, and move on to Houdini-like escapism and physical endurance. David's next special would be no mere magic show, as he intended to duplicate one of Houdini's most famous feats.

BURIED ALIVE

David first came up with the idea of burying himself alive in 1998. Ever since he was a kid, he had practiced going without food and had developed the ability to enter a trance-like state to conserve air and energy. Rather than burying himself under dirt, however, David wanted to be buried in a clear plastic coffin underneath a six-foot, water-filled Plexiglas tank. His goal was to remain there seven days, something no magician had ever accomplished. He purchased a coffin and trained himself by staying inside of it for up to four days at a time.

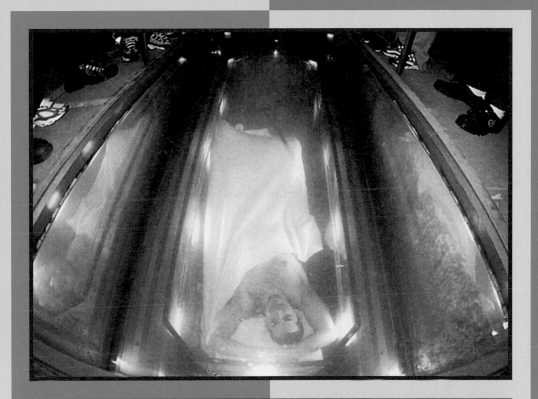

David is buried six feet underground in a clear coffin beneath a three-ton plastic water tank of his own design, planning to stay there for seven days. David's "Buried Alive" stunt was an homage to fellow magician Harry Houdini, who died before trying this type of feat.

On Monday, April 5, 1999, David entered the tomb and began the exhausting feat. As he later recalled in his book, it was more difficult than he thought it would be.

> **"I expected the burial to be only slightly harder than lying on my living room couch. I couldn't have been more wrong. . . . [Once] I was sealed in the coffin . . . I realized that training in the living room didn't help me one iota. I immediately panicked. . . . The first sixty minutes were sheer hell."**

To make matters worse, early on he thought there was a problem with his oxygen supply, and throughout the entire seven days of the event he had to **endure** flashbulbs from cameras and laser pointers from skeptics believing that he wasn't really in the coffin. The biggest obstacle he faced, though, was his own physical limit. By the third day, David described feeling "aches and pains in places I didn't even know existed." He ate nothing, and only drank four tablespoons of water per day.

AFTER THE BURIAL

An estimated 75,000 people visited the site of David's living burial during the week-long stunt. Among them was Marie Blood, the niece of the great Harry Houdini. Marie was impressed by David's performance, telling *The New York Post*,

> "My uncle did some amazing things, but he could not have done this . . . he wouldn't have had the patience that David showed."

At the end of the seventh day, David was brought back to the surface. He was weak, and he had lost two dozen pounds in the process, but he had successfully completed the amazing feat. He was examined by medical experts, who said he was in good health. Afterward, David says the first thing he did was take a three-hour bubble bath, but it wasn't too long before he started plotting his next test of endurance.

FROZEN IN TIME

For his next stunt, David, who by this time had earned the nickname "The Hip-Hop Houdini," promised to do something very cool. What started off as a planned attempt to duplicate Houdini's Chinese Water Torture Cell feat changed drastically when David realized how much the chamber looked like a block of ice. This was an incredibly difficult and medically risky stunt. David would be putting himself at risk for shock, hypothermia, and a host of other potential health problems. As he later wrote in his book,

David peers through the walls of a six-ton block of ice, which would be his temporary home during his next feat. He created the event for an ABC TV special, which documented David's emergence from the icy prison on November 29, 2000, after a 58-hour stay.

Calling his 2002 challenge "Vertigo," David stands atop an 80-foot pillar in Bryant Park in New York City. After balancing there for 35 hours, he was exhausted and dehydrated, but David said he felt lucky to be in a business where he could entertain people with such a fantastic stunt.

❝I was well aware of these dangers, but I was still determined to go ahead with the ice endurance challenge. People are always asking me why I do these things to myself. I don't really have a concise answer to that question. . . . I know that when I push myself to the absolute limit, I feel more alive than ever.**❞**

In November 2000, David did indeed go through with the stunt. He spent 63 hours, 42 minutes and 15 seconds frozen inside a giant block of ice in the middle of Times Square, New York. As expected, the performance took an incredible physical toll on him. Despite having spent months training, he eventually began experiencing hallucinations and started behaving abnormally as his then-girlfriend, model Josie Maran, and many others watched. At the end of the stunt, David was removed from the ice with a chain saw and rushed to the hospital.

Later, David admitted that he couldn't walk for a month. Though he was disappointed because his physical condition kept him from speaking afterward and dedicating the stunt to his mother, he was pleased by the positive reaction to Frozen in Time. He called the media coverage "intense" and noted that legions of fans followed along thanks to a live, online feed. The feat might have taken its toll on David, but it also ensured that the "Hip-Hop Houdini" would join Criss Angel as one of the world's elite performers.

HEIGHTS, HEARTS, AND HARDCOVER BOOKS

Roughly two years after the Frozen in Time performance, 29-year-old David returned to public attention in a big way, with a stunt known as Vertigo. In May 2002, he spent 35 hours standing on top of an 80-foot tall pillar in New York's Bryant Park. Afterward, he jumped off the structure into a stack of cardboard boxes, a leap that was shown live on national TV. Once again, the feat took a physical toll on him, leaving him sleep deprived, dehydrated and physically sore. However, as he later wrote, it was all definitely worth it.

Criss Angel

Like David Blaine, Criss Angel is a magician and endurance performer. In fact, some writers have suggested that the two are rivals. Criss was born Christopher Nicholas Sarantakos on December 19, 1967, and was raised on Long Island, New York. He is the star of the popular television show *Criss Angel: Mindfreak*, which currently airs on the A&E television network and is about to enter its fifth season.

Criss has also recently teamed up with Cirque de Soleil to create a live show in Las Vegas called *Criss Angel: Believe*. Over the years, he has performed many well-known illusions, including walking on water, levitating above a hotel, making an automobile disappear, being run over by a steamroller, getting cut in half, and surviving in an exploding crate. Also, in 2007, he wrote a book, *Mindfreak: Secret Revelations*.

“Once again, I returned to my home from a challenge so banged up I couldn't even walk through the front door on my own. But it was nice to realize just how fortunate I am to be in the business of taking my wildest dreams and fantasies and turning them into realities.”

Vertigo wasn't the only trick David had up his sleeve in 2002. Also during the month of May, he appeared on *Last Call with Carson Daly* and performed an illusion so intense and realistic that it almost didn't make it to air. During the appearance, he appeared to pull his heart out of his chest, reportedly sending members of the audience fleeing in tears.

Finally, in October, his book, *Mysterious Stanger: A Book of Magic* was published. The book was part **autobiography**, part history of magic, and part how-to manual. It also featured a real-life contest with $100,000 going to the winner. The contest was created by award-winning game designer Cliff Johnson, and was solved by a reader about 16 months after the book's release. With a pair of noteworthy performances and a popular book to his credit over the year, 2002 was definitely a magical time for David.

ABOVE THE BELOW

David's next major test of endurance, Above the Below, came in September 2003. For this feat, he would enter a clear Plexiglas cage that was suspended 30 feet above the famous River Thames in London. Once locked inside the case, David would get no food and under five liters of water per day. As with many of

David sits in a glass cage above the River Thames in London in 2003. David's stunt, in which he spent 44 days in the box without food, left him dangerously malnourished. However, even after a hospital stay he was eager to move on to his next amazing feat.

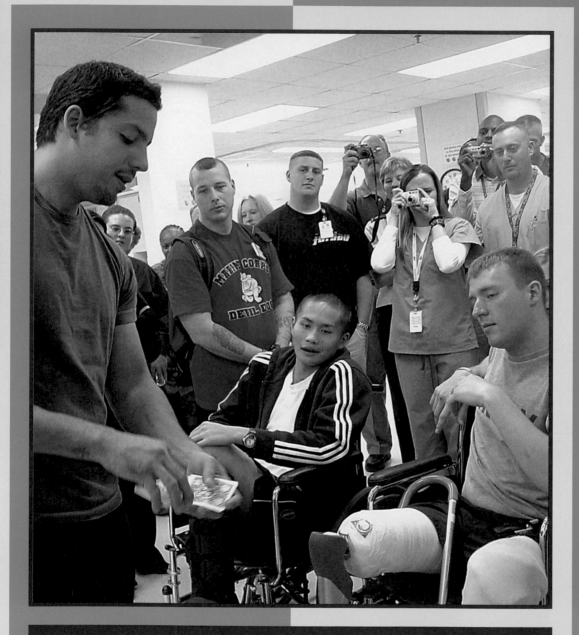

David returns to his love of street magic as he performs sleight of hand for wounded soldiers at an army medical center in 2005. It means a lot to David to give his time to good causes; he entertained veterans at the hospital twice more with his prestidigitation.

his previous stunts, there were concerns over David's health, particularly possible malnutrition and the risks he faced once he started eating again.

Again, David took all the concerns in stride and started the feat on the fifth day of the month. He remained there, fasting, for a total of 44 days. In addition to severe pain, David had to deal with emotional abuse from critics and hecklers. Some threw eggs at him. One person tried to cut off his water supply, while another taunted him by dangling a hamburger outside the case. Yet David endured and managed to overcome it all. Despite losing 50 pounds in the process, he emerged from the case victorious on October 19.

PURSUING OTHER ACTIVITIES

After spending a few weeks in the hospital, David announced his next planned stunt: jumping into a river from a helicopter thousands of feet in the air. However, the event, which had been planned for April 2004, never happened. Still, David found ways to keep busy. The man who once had reportedly dated Madonna, actress Daryl Hannah, and musician Bijou Phillips had since been romantically linked to models Manon Von Gerkan and Lucy Clarkson.

On November 22, 2005, David returned to the world of prestidigitation, as he performed sleight of hand and card tricks for wounded soldiers at the Brooke Army Medical Center in Texas. He was so moved by the experience that he returned to the hospital two more times. Clearly, he had made good use of his time out of the limelight. However, the "Hip-Hop Houdini" obviously still had several more feats of physical endurance in him—not to mention a world record or two.

STILL WORKING HIS MAGIC

THOUGH HE HAD NEVER FULLY GOTTEN away from the craft, 2006 marked David's triumphant return to the world of performance magic in many ways. That year, he performed his first major stunt in nearly three years, continued using his talents to give back to the community, earned a place in the record books, and found the love of his life.

In May 2006, he planned a performance that would feature two incredible feats in one. The stunt was called Drowned Alive, and would begin with the now 33-year-old David being placed into an eight-foot-diameter sphere filled with water. He would be connected to a special breathing device and be placed in 2,000 gallons of salt water for seven days. If all went well during the first part, he would then remove his breathing tube and try to break the world record for breath holding.

David is still working his magic as he performs his "Drowned Alive" stunt in New York in 2006. Although he wasn't able to set a breath-holding record, David did stay underwater in an eight-foot-diameter bubble for an unbelievable seven days.

DROWNED ALIVE

David practiced for the event by holding his breath for 48 minutes every hour, letting more time pass between each breath. He also trained with Navy SEALs to help develop both physical and mental endurance underwater. On May 1, in front of the Lincoln Center in New York, he donned gloves filled with petroleum jelly for protection, was hooked up to water and feeding tubes, entered the sphere, and was lowered into the water. Thus the stunt began, and it was time to see how well his training had paid off.

Navy SEALs

In preparation for his Drowned Alive stunt, David trained with the United States Navy Sea, Air, and Land forces, better known as the SEALs. He chose wisely. Members of this elite special operations force have to undergo strict and difficult training to prepare for their missions, which typically include underwater demolition, special recon, counter-terrorism, anti-drug missions, and personnel recovery.

The Navy SEALs began training in 1943 and were officially activated in 1962. It is believed that they were an answer to the Army's own elite force, the Green Berets. They have been involved in the Vietnam War, Operation Desert Storm, and Operation Iraqi Freedom, and have also worked during hijackings. In early 2009 SEALs played a key role in combating modern-day pirates from Somalia.

Early on, things went well for David, as he told ABC News after the first 20 hours,

> **"The only difficulty I have been having is that my hands are already mangled and my feet are pretty bad. It feels like pins and needles, and the flesh is starting to get little perforations. . . . I almost feel guilty doing it. It feels so good to be in here."**

It would get much worse, though. David remained submerged for 177 hours, and over time the conditions took their toll on his body. Not only did the water started to eat away at the skin on his hands and feet, but doctors also started to have concerns about possible liver failure and other health problems. Still, he managed to endure the entire seven days underwater. David's health issues prevented him from setting the record on this occasion, but he would have another chance later on down the road.

REVOLUTION

Throughout his career, David's magic had not only given him pleasure and brought enjoyment to thousands of people, but it had also made him quite famous and well off financially. With the money he made from the Drowned Alive stunt, David was able to not only purchase a $1.67 million apartment in TriBeCa, a neighborhood in lower Manhattan, but also turn his attention to helping out the less fortunate.

In November 2006, David teamed with the Salvation Army and the Target chain of retail stores for his next feat of endurance,

David is attached to a gyroscope 40 feet above the ground as he begins his stunt "Revolution" in New York's Times Square during Thanksgiving week, 2006. Teaming up with Target and the Salvation Army, David created the event to offer needy children a holiday shopping spree.

called Revolution. On the Tuesday before Thanksgiving, David would be shackled to a **gyroscope** device 40 feet above Times Square. The gyroscope would then start spinning and rotate eight times per minute. David's mission was to escape before Target's special holiday sale began at 6 A.M. on Friday of that week.

David braved cold, hunger, and thirst but escaped from the gyroscope in time to take 100 children shopping at Target, November 24, 2006. He was thrilled that Target's challenge helped so many deserving youngsters and felt he had spent a very fulfilling Thanksgiving.

Once again, he faced danger. No shield would protect him from rain, snow, extreme cold, or other weather elements, and he would be unable to eat or drink anything for the duration of the event. Still, he was determined to go through with it, since the Salvation Army had helped his family growing up, giving them clothing when they needed it most. He saw this as an opportunity to give back.

A SPECIAL THANKSGIVING

At 10 A.M., David was strapped into the gyroscope, and the stunt began. As it rotated, David fought to free himself from his chains, all the while dodging a chilly rain. Making the feat even more difficult was the extreme hunger and thirst that eventually set in. However, David was determined and kept at it. Finally, at 2:15 P.M. on Thursday, he managed to work himself free and fell to the ground. Afterwards, an exhausted David told reporters that the feat was harder than he had expected, but added he couldn't be happier with the result.

> **❝I am thrilled that the challenge is over and that 100 children will receive a dream holiday shopping spree tomorrow at Target. This has been an amazing experience and I could not have spent my Thanksgiving in a more fulfilling way.❞**

The following day at 5 A.M., one hour before the doors opened, David led 100 needy children on a $500 shopping spree at a Target store in Jersey City, New Jersey. It was a storybook ending to the entire Thanksgiving event, and Target Vice President of Marketing John Remington was extremely thankful for David's participation.

> **❝There's absolutely no one else who can grab the public's attention like David Blaine. Target is thankful that he accepted our challenge and succeeded in time to join the children and their families. . . . With David's help, this should be a wonderful and unforgettable season for all.❞**

DOING GOOD AND CHASING DREAMS

Revolution was far from the only thing David did in 2006. That summer, he had helped kick off the New York Public Library's Summer Reading Program. Later, he visited Israel and performed

David continues his charitable work as he entertains children at Maimonides Medical Center in Brooklyn, New York. From helping kick off a summer reading program to performing magic for families in shelters in Israel, David finds it rewarding to give back to the community.

for both kids and injured soldiers at various locations. Then on December 13, David visited the Maimonides Infants & Children's Hospital in Brooklyn. There he entertained patients with card tricks and other feats of prestidigitation. Such works were undoubtedly rewarding, but deep down, David remained driven to break the breath-holding record.

On April 30, 2008, he finally was able to have another chance. Appearing on *The Oprah Winfrey Show*, David managed to hold his breath for more than 17 minutes, officially setting the world record in the breath-holding category. David later called it "a life-long dream," which was a fitting reward to someone who had been working hard over the past few years to help make the dreams of so many others come true. David wasn't finished yet, though. Before the end of 2008, he would participate in yet another major stunt.

Other Famous Celebrities on *Oprah*

The Oprah Winfrey Show, which debuted nationally in September 1986, is the longest-running and highest-rated daytime talk show in U.S. television history. *Time* magazine once called it one of the best shows of the 20th century, and *TV Guide* ranked it as one of the top 50 American television programs of all time.

One of the reasons for the show's success has been the numerous celebrity guests that have appeared on the program. They have provided some of the show's most memorable moments, including the famous Tom Cruise couch-jumping incident, as well as an interview with Elizabeth Taylor that Oprah has called the toughest of her career. Other stars who have appeared on the show over the years include Bono, Ashton Kutcher, Demi Moore, Chris Rock, Ben Stiller, Hugh Jackman, Tom Hanks, Jennifer Aniston, and Sean Penn.

DIVE OF DEATH

On September 18, 2008, David and Donald Trump joined forces at a press conference outside Trump Tower in New York City to announce David's next stunt. He would hang upside down in Central Park for 60 hours with no safety net beneath him. At the end of the stunt, in a two-hour televised special, he would leap off the support structure and then be pulled up and away into the atmosphere by hot-air balloons.

However, some people cried foul when, during the stunt, David was spotted by several news media outlets standing rightside up, drinking water and receiving medical attention. Yet as Patrick Smith, one of David's agents, told the Web site Gawker.com, that had actually been the plan since day one.

> **"In all of his discussions with the media, [David] said he would have to occasionally get his head above his heart and lower his legs to correct circulation. . . . His doctors told him quite simply that if he didn't correct blood flow, he could die. . . . Enjoy the spectacle. It's free. And give the guy a break."**

Even though there were legitimate medical reasons for the breaks, they still hurt the public perception of David's Dive of Death stunt. Making things worse, the ending had to be altered at the last minute due to weather conditions and did not come off as well as initially hoped. The TV special also featured David performing a bullet catch and once again taking a page out of Houdini's book by having mixed martial arts fighter Kimbo Slice punch him in the stomach. However, it was seen by just 7.7 million people and finished third in its time slot.

MORE TRICKS UP HIS SLEEVE

Undaunted by his critics, David continues to perform magic and plan feats of endurance. On December 23, 2008, he participated in a New York area coat drive, donating the coat off his back and later signing autographs and chatting with other volunteers. On his birthday, April 4, 2009, David worked his magic in a different way. On that date, the magician proposed to his supermodel girlfriend, Alizee Guinochet.

Having completed so many incredible feats, one has to wonder what is left for David Blaine to accomplish. After all, he has survived being buried alive. He has lived after being frozen in a

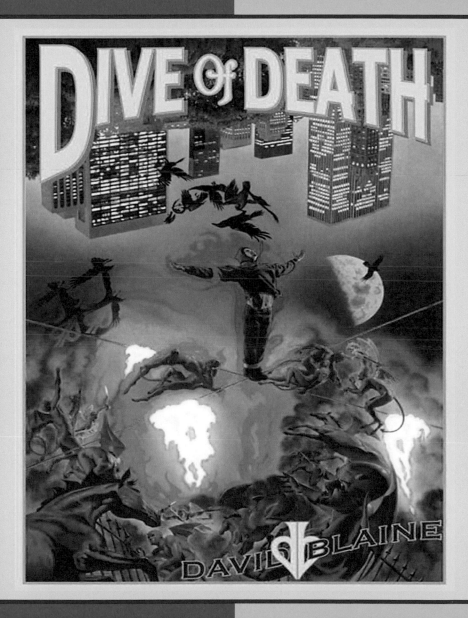

David's 2008 feat, "Dive of Death," included hanging upside down for 60 hours. He was criticized for taking breaks during the event and had to change the ending because of the weather. But David finished the TV special more confident than ever and went on to plan his next performance.

After feats of endurance like being buried alive, frozen in ice, and submerged underwater for days at a time, David still has more amazing stunts to perform. His fans look forward to seeing whatever future tricks he has up his sleeve as he continues to amaze audiences with his gift of magic.

Alizee Guinochet

In April 2009, several different New York area newspapers and Web sites broke the news that David Blaine had become engaged to 23-year-old model Alizee Guinochet. Later in April, *New York Post* reporter Lawrence Schwartzwald noted that they were both wearing matching pre-engagement rings, and that David had promised to buy her a fancier engagement ring once the economy improved.

Alizee is a 23-year-old French model who was born on May 17, 1986. She has appeared in the magazines *Elle* and *Cosmogirl*, been featured in print ads for the Saks department store, and also participated in the 2004 Ready to Wear Fall/Winter fashion show. According to what an unnamed friend of David's told usmagazine.com, Alizee is a "great girl . . . smart and talented." As of May 1, 2009, no wedding date had been announced.

block of ice. He has set a world record for holding his breath and has freed himself from a spinning gyroscope to benefit the less fortunate. David will undoubtedly try to cheat death many more times during his life. After all, as he once told the British newspaper *The Guardian*, he's not afraid of what could happen.

> **"I think if I was afraid of death I wouldn't be able to live my life because my mother passed away in my arms. . . . I look at it as poetic, because she was so peaceful. . . . If I looked at it any other way, since I loved her so much, it would be difficult for me to accept the beauty of the world."**

While we don't know for sure what stunt David Blaine will come up with next, we can be sure of one thing. Whatever it happens to be, it will undoubtedly be a feat that is truly magical.

1973   David Blaine White is born on April 4 in Brooklyn, New York, to William Perez, of Italian and Puerto Rican descent, and Patrice Maureen White, a Jew of Russian descent.

1977   David's father leaves the family.

1983   David's mother marries John Bukalo; the family relocates to Little Falls, New Jersey.

1995   David's mother passes away from cancer; David begins focusing on his street magic career.

1997   His first TV special, *David Blaine: Street Magic*, airs on May 19 on the ABC television network.

1999   David's second TV special, *David Blaine: Magic Man*, is broadcast on ABC.

He completes his Buried Alive stunt from April 5 through April 12.

2000   In November, for his Frozen in Time feat, David is encased in a giant block of ice in the middle of Times Square, New York.

2002   David stands on top of a pillar in Bryant Park, New York, for 35 hours during his Vertigo stunt.

At the end of the Vertigo stunt, he jumped off the 80-foot tall building onto a pile of cardboard boxes.

Later on that year, David's book, *Mysterious Stranger: A Book of Magic* is published. The book is part autobiography, part history of magic, part how-to manual, and part real-life contest, with $100,000 going to the first person to solve a riddle contained within the book.

2003   On September 5, David begins his Above the Below stunt, during which he spent 44 days inside a Plexiglas cage suspended above the River Thames in London. Despite some taunting from the crowd, he is successful and leaves the box on October 19.

2004   California native Sherry Skanes, a school teacher, solves the riddle in *Mysterious Stranger: A Book of Magic* on March 24 and wins the $100,000 prize.

2006 On May 1, David begins his Drowned Alive stunt. He remains underwater inside a protective sphere for seven days, then tries—and fails—to set a new record for breath-holding at the end of the event.

In November, David teams up with the Salvation Army and the Target chain of retail stores for a charity event called Revolution. David escapes from a moving gyroscope, and in doing so, earns $500 gift cards for 100 lucky kids.

2008 On April 30, David appears on *The Oprah Winfrey Show* and manages to break the world record for breath-holding, doing so for more than 17 minutes.

Later on, in September of that year, he begins his controversial Dive of Death stunt. Despite a few problems and some criticism, the magician managed to hang upside-down for 60 hours and the stunt was featured as part of a two-hour television special.

2009 David becomes engaged to girlfriend Alizee Guinochet on his birthday, April 4.

Awards and Nominations

2000   Nominated for British Video Association and Home Entertainment Weekly awards for his DVD *Mystifier*.

2008   Set a world record by holding his breath for 17 minutes, 4 seconds.

Nominated for the first ever Houdini Award.

Television Specials

1997   *David Blaine: Street Magic*

1999   *David Blaine: Magic Man*

2000   *David Blaine: Frozen in Time*

2002   *David Blaine: Fearless*

David Blaine: Vertigo

2003   *David Blaine: Above the Below*

2006   *David Blaine: Drowned Alive*

2008   *The Oprah Winfrey Show* (breath-holding record attempt)

David Blaine: Dive of Death

aspire—to have something as a goal; to want to achieve something.

astonishment—a feeling of wonder or amazement.

autobiography—a book in which the author tells his or her own life story.

enamored—fascinated by; intensely drawn to.

endure—to overcome obstacles or hardship through determination or hard work.

gyroscope—a spinning wheel, usually used in measurement, that moves in all directions.

manipulate—to change or have control over something.

legerdemain—a French word for stage magic that literally means "lightness of hand."

levitation—lifting a person or thing in a way that seems supernatural.

posthumously—after a person's death.

prestidigitation—another word for stage magic that literally means "quick fingers."

saturate—filled to the maximum level.

submerged—placed under water.

surpass—to become better than; to achieve more than.

undaunted—not discouraged by; showing courage in the face of difficulties or criticism.

Books

Blaine, David. *Mysterious Stranger: A Book of Magic*. New York: Villard, 2003.

Christopher, Milbourne and Maurine Christopher. *The Illustrated History of Magic*. New York: Running Press, 2005.

Haskins, James and Kathleen Benson. *Conjure Times: Black Magicians in America*. New York: Walker and Company, 2001.

Ogden, Tom. *The Complete Idiot's Guide to Street Magic*. New York: Penguin, 2007.

Pogue, David. *Magic for Dummies*. New York: Hungry Minds, 1998.

Web Sites

http://www.davidblaine.com/

This is the official Web site for the "Hip-Hop Houdini." It contains news updates, photos showing fans what David has been up to, and videos of some of his most memorable performances, including several clips of him performing street magic.

http://www.magicdirectory.com/blaine/

Not only does this outstanding Web site feature a nice David Blaine bio, but it also has loads of information about some of his earlier stunts, including Above the Below, Buried Alive, Frozen in Time, and Vertigo.

http://www.learnmagictricks.org/

Want to be the next David Blaine? Well, you may not be able to become a master escape artist or hold your breath for 17 minutes, but the free videos on this Web site will show you how to perform card tricks, coin tricks, and other feats of prestidigitation.

page

2: ABC Network/NMI	**31:** ABC Network/NMI
6: LOC/PRMM	**32:** Yariv Milchan/Magic Magazine/PRMS
9: George Burns/Harpo Productions Inc.	**35:** James Spector/IOA
10: George Burns/Harpo Productions Inc.	**37:** Zuma Press
13: George Burns/Harpo Productions Inc.	**38:** James Spector/IOA
15: Retna	**41:** James Spector/IOA
15: (insert) ABC Network/NMI	**42:** UPI Photos
17: WirePix/FPS	**45:** Joe Benjamin/IOA
18: Jamie Beeden/Sky Magazine	**47:** Mark Von Holden/Target/PRNS
21: New Millennium Images	**48:** Mark Von Holden/Target/PRNS
22: New Millennium Images	**50:** DINO212/PRNS
25: New Millennium Images	**53:** New Millennium Images
27: New Millennium Images	**54:** Abaca/KRT
28: WirePix/FPS	

Front cover: Zuma Press

Chuck Bednar is an author and freelance writer from Ohio. He has been writing professionally since 1997 and has written more than 1,500 published nonfiction articles. Bednar is the author of eight books, including the *Tony Parker* and *Tim Duncan* entries in Mason Crest's MODERN ROLE MODELS series, as well as SUPERSTARS OF PRO FOOTBALL: *Tony Romo*. He is currently employed by Bright Hub (www.brighthub.com) as the Managing Editor for their Nintendo Wii Web site.